D1276297

The Bizarre Life Cycle of a CUCKOO

By Barbara M. Linde

Gareth Stevens
Publishing

Please visit our website, www.garethstevens.com. For a free color catalog of all our high-quality books, call toll free 1-800-542-2595 or fax 1-877-542-2596.

Library of Congress Cataloging-in-Publication Data

Linde, Barbara M.
The bizarre life cycle of a cuckoo / Barbara M. Linde.
    p. cm. — (Strange life cycles)
Includes index.
ISBN 978-1-4339-7044-3 (pbk.)
ISBN 978-1-4339-7045-0 (6-pack)
ISBN 978-1-4339-7043-6 (library binding)
1. Cuckoos—Life cycles—Juvenile literature. I. Title.
QL696.C83L56 2013
598.7'4—dc23
                        2012000271

First Edition

Published in 2013 by
Gareth Stevens Publishing
111 East 14th Street, Suite 349
New York, NY 10003

Copyright © 2013 Gareth Stevens Publishing

Designer: Andrea Davison-Bartolotta
Editor: Kristen Rajczak

Photo credits: Cover, p. 1 Hagit Berkovich/Shutterstock.com; pp. 4, 9, 14, 21 (bottom) Florian Andronache/Shutterstock.com; p. 5 © iStockphoto.com/Andy Gehrig; p. 7 G. Ronald Austing/Photo Researchers/Getty Images; pp. 11, 21 (top) George Reszeter/Oxford Scientific/Getty Images; p. 13, 21 (right) Stockbyte/Thinkstock; pp. 15, 19 Jonathan Gale/Oxford Scientific/Getty Images; p. 16 iStockphoto/Thinkstock; p. 17 © iStockphoto.com/Raymond Pauly; p. 20 Maksimilian/Shutterstock.com; p. 21 (center) Alenka M/Shutterstock.com; p. 21 (left) RazvanZinica/Shutterstock.com.

Printed in the United States of America

CPSIA compliance information: Batch #CS12GS: For further information contact Gareth Stevens, New York, New York at 1-800-542-2595.

Contents

Words in the glossary appear in **bold** type the first time they are used in the text.

What Is a Cuckoo?

A cuckoo is a kind of bird. The smallest cuckoos are about 6.5 inches (16.5 cm) long, while larger cuckoos may be up to 36 inches (91 cm) long. Cuckoos don't look strange. Soft feathers cover their wings, body, and long tail. Their beak curves down. A cuckoo has two legs and two feet. Each foot has four toes.

Although cuckoos don't look odd, some kinds have strange habits. They don't build a nest for their eggs. That's because they lay their eggs in other birds' nests!

THE FACTS OF LIFE

The cuckoo's call sounds like its name: "cu-coo." The male bird sings this song to **attract** a female bird.

When flying, cuckoos beat their wings quickly for a little while, and then they **glide**.

Building Nests

There are many different types of cuckoos. Some of them, such as the yellow-billed cuckoo, build nests and **hatch** their own young. A male and female yellow-billed cuckoo **mate** and build a nest made of twigs and grass.

The female lays up to five eggs. Then, the male and female yellow-billed cuckoos take care of the eggs together. After about 10 days, the eggs hatch. The parents feed the babies. In about 7 days, the chicks are grown enough to leave the nest.

THE **FACTS** OF **LIFE**

Baby cuckoos start to get their feathers about 6 days after they hatch.

The yellow-billed cuckoo builds its nest hidden in a tree or bush that isn't too high off the ground.

7

Borrowing Nests

Some kinds of cuckoos have a much stranger idea of parenting. They don't raise their own babies. Instead, the female lays her eggs in the nests of other birds! These kinds of cuckoos are called brood parasites.

First, the cuckoo makes a fuss so the **host** mother bird will leave her nest. The cuckoo may push the host's eggs out of the nest or even eat one to make room for her egg. Then, the cuckoo lays her egg in its place.

THE FACTS OF LIFE

A brood is a group of young birds that hatch together. A parasite is an animal that depends on another animal without giving it anything in return.

The cuckoo lays one egg in each of several different nests.

Look-Alike Eggs

Over time, cuckoos have found ways to make sure their eggs are cared for. The cuckoo's eggs **mimic** the host bird's eggs, though they may be larger. Sometimes, the host bird recognizes the cuckoo's egg and leaves it to start a new nest. More often, the host bird sits on all the eggs.

The cuckoo egg hatches first, sometimes a whole day before the other eggs. This is because a cuckoo mother holds the egg in her body a day longer than other birds.

THE FACTS OF LIFE

The female cuckoo lays her eggs in the nests of the same kind of bird that raised her.

The cuckoo's egg is larger than the reed warbler's and a slightly different color. However, the mother reed warbler will take care of it.

Caring for the Visitor

The hungry cuckoo chick mimics the cries of the host mother bird's own babies so the mother will feed it. The baby cuckoo tosses other eggs or chicks out of the nest to get more food. Even then, the host mother still feeds the cuckoo!

A young cuckoo eats whatever the host mother gives it. This may be beetles, grasshoppers, or fruit. Once the chick is old enough, it leaves the nest. It then **migrates** to the same place as its cuckoo parents.

THE FACTS OF LIFE

Host mothers continue to feed cuckoo chicks even when the chicks become much larger than the host bird!

A cape batis feeds a growing cuckoo.

13

On the Move

When young cuckoos born in cold areas are old enough, they migrate. The cuckoo's strange life cycle doesn't stop after the chicks leave the nest. They also have a weird ability to follow their cuckoo parents without any directions!

Cuckoos fly to warmer areas for the winter and then fly back again. Some stay within one country. Others fly thousands of miles across land or oceans. They often fly nonstop for weeks at a time.

THE FACTS OF LIFE

Cuckoos in England migrate 4,000 miles (6,436 km) to Africa and back again every year.

Cuckoos have strong wings to help them fly long distances.

15

Worldwide Habitat

Cuckoos mate when they are old enough, and the life cycle starts again. Cuckoos live all over the world. For some, their **habitat** is a deep forest. Others live in **orchards** or empty fields. Cuckoos can be found in both cold and warm **climates**.

Some kinds of cuckoos like trees, and some kinds like to stay on the ground. Cuckoos commonly live alone, though. They hide so well in their habitats, it's more common to hear a cuckoo call out "cu-coo" than to see the bird.

roadrunner

THE FACTS OF LIFE

One kind of cuckoo, the roadrunner, lives in the deserts of the southwestern United States. It can run up to 17 miles (27 km) per hour.

This squirrel cuckoo can be found in Central America.

Skillful Hunters

Cuckoo chicks are brought food by their parents or host mothers. Adult cuckoos are insect hunters. Hairy caterpillars are a favorite cuckoo food. Luckily for the cuckoos, most other birds don't eat these caterpillars!

To catch a caterpillar, the cuckoo sits on a branch. It watches the grass and leaves below. When a caterpillar moves, the cuckoo pounces. Snap! It grabs the caterpillar in its beak. The cuckoo shakes and rolls the caterpillar, then swallows it whole!

THE FACTS OF LIFE

Cuckoos in the Caribbean Islands eat lizards. That's why they're called lizard cuckoos!

A cuckoo with a hairy caterpillar in its beak is ready for a meal.

19

Cuckoos in Danger

Some cuckoos are **endangered**. They face problems in many parts of their life cycle. When habitats are cut down, the host birds have nowhere to live. Then the cuckoo mother has nowhere to lay her eggs. Migrating is harder as deserts grow bigger and hotter. Farmers put poisons on their crops to kill pests, and cuckoos have fewer bugs and caterpillars to eat.

Now some people are helping keep the cuckoos safe. We don't want the "cu-coo" of the cuckoo to be silent forever.

A cuckoo's feathers help it blend in with its habitat.

The Life Cycle of a Cuckoo

Cuckoo eggs are laid in a nest.

Adult cuckoos mate.

Cuckoo chicks are cared for by their parents or a host bird.

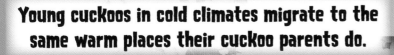

Young cuckoos in cold climates migrate to the same warm places their cuckoo parents do.

Glossary

attract: to draw toward

climate: the average weather conditions of a place over a period of time

endangered: in danger of dying out

glide: to move with smooth and quiet motion

habitat: the natural place where an animal or plant lives

hatch: to break open or come out of

host: an animal or plant that provides for another kind of animal or plant

mate: to come together to make babies

migrate: to move from one area to another for feeding or having babies

mimic: to look or sound like someone or something else

orchard: a field full of fruit trees

For More Information

Books

Bredeson, Carmen. *Weird Birds*. Berkeley Heights, NJ: Enslow Publishers, 2010.

Patchett, Fiona. *Eggs and Chicks*. Tulsa, OK: EDC Publishing, 2006.

Websites

Cuckoos and Relatives
www.biokids.umich.edu/critters/Cuculiformes/
Read more about cuckoos, see pictures, and listen to their call.

Yellow-Billed Cuckoo
www.nhptv.org/wild/yellowbilledcuckoo.asp
Find out more about this cuckoo's interesting life.

Publisher's note to educators and parents: Our editors have carefully reviewed these websites to ensure that they are suitable for students. Many websites change frequently, however, and we cannot guarantee that a site's future contents will continue to meet our high standards of quality and educational value. Be advised that students should be closely supervised whenever they access the Internet.

Index